# Masters of the Violin

### Edited by Gabriel Banat

### VOLUME 6

### Works for the Violin

*Michel Corrette* 1709- 1795

[Works, instrumental. Selections]

### Introduction by Edith Borroff

### Performance Notes by Gabriel Banat

mc
410
c82
1982

25648

### *Johnson Reprint Corporation*

Ⓡ

# Masters of the Violin

### Edited by Gabriel Banat

VOLUME 6

### Works for the Violin

*Michel Corrette* 1709-1795

[Works, instrumental. Selections]

### Introduction by Edith Borroff

### Performance Notes by Gabriel Banat

*Johnson Reprint Corporation*
*Harcourt Brace Jovanovich, Publishers*

In order to preserve the authentic character of the works in this volume, no editing or alteration of the original document has been permitted. Suggestions regarding performance practices of the period as well as a list of errata have been included to make this music accessible for modern use.

Johnson Reprint Corporation
757 Third Avenue, New York, New York 10017

United Kingdom Edition published by
Johnson Reprint, Ltd.
24-28 Oval Road, London NW1 7DX

Michel Corrette: Six Symphonies en Quatuor contenant les plus beaux Noëls François et Etrangers avec des Variations. Reproduced by permission of the Bibliothèque Municipale, Lille.

Michel Corrette: Le Mirliton. I<sup>R.</sup> Concerto Comique. Oeuvre Rés.F.50 et 50 bis, micr. Bibl. nat., Paris. Reproduced by permission of the Bibliothèque Nationale, Paris.

Michel Corrette: Le Quadrille, IV<sup>E</sup> Concerto Comique. Oeuvre Rés.F.53 et 53 bis, micr. Bibl. nat., Paris. Reproduced by permission of the Bibliothèque Nationale, Paris.

Michel Corrette: La Servante au Bon Tabac. VII. Concerto Comique. Oeuvre Rés.F.55 et 55 bis, micr. Bibl. nat., Paris. Reproduced by permission of the Bibliothèque Nationale, Paris.

Michel Corrette: Les Pantins. XVII<sup>e.</sup> Concerto Comique. K.5.c.11. Reproduced by permission of the British Library.

Michel Corrette: La Touriere. XVIII. Concerto Comique. h.303.c. Reproduced by permission of the British Library.

Michel Corrette: XIX Concerto Comique, Contenant La Turque Et La Confession. Oeuvre Rés.F.65 et 65 bis, micr. Bibl. nat., Paris. Reproduced by permission of the Bibliothèque Nationale, Paris.

Michel Corrette: XXIV Concerto Comique contenant La Marche du Huron. h.303.d. Reproduced by permission of the British Library.

Michel Corrette: Les Sauvages et la Furstemberg. XXV Concerto Comique. K.5.c.12. Reproduced by permission of the British Library.

Michel Corrette: VI Duetti, À Due Violini, ò à Flauti traversi. Opera XXIII<sup>a</sup>. Reproduced by permission of the British Library.

Michel Corrette: Sonates pour le Clavecin avec un Accompagnement de Violon. Opera XXV. Oeuvre Rés.F.889, micr. Bibl. nat., Paris. Reproduced by permission of the Bibliothèque Nationale, Paris.

Library of Congress Catalog Number: 81-80306

First reprinting, 1982

Printed in the United States of America

ISBN: 0-384-03186-2

# MICHEL CORRETTE

## Edith Borroff
The State University of New York at Binghamton

Michel Corrette was one of the most active musicians during a time when musical activity in Paris was at a height—a height unprecedented there and elsewhere. His energy must have been prodigious and sustained, for he enjoyed a varied musical career that extended through eight decades; he was a musical force from the late 1720s well into the 1780s, thus spanning the greater part of the eighteenth century.

Virtually nothing is known of Corrette's life but the bare outline. He was born in 1709, in Rouen, where his father, Gaspard, was an organist. Gaspard Corrette, a Dutchman born in Delft, was a proponent of the Italian style; his publication for the organ of 1703 is considered the first to present a strong Italian component in French music for that instrument. Called to Paris consoles while Michel was a toddler, Gaspard was the organist at Saint-Denis-et-Saint-Jean in 1712. It was in the Paris of the 1720s, then, that Michel Corrette was formed as a musician. He was sixteen when the Concert spirituel was organized and nineteen when in 1726 he took his first important console at Sainte-Marie-Madeleine. By the age of twenty-six he was married and had already begun his intense activity as a teacher and composer.[1] At thirty he was organist to the Grand Prieur de France and had already published his violin and flute methods. He maintained his position as an organist at the Grand Collège des Jésuites in 1750, then for the Prince de Condé from 1759, and for the Duc d'Angoulême in 1780. His creative work continued into his eighties: the *Chaconne du tiers-état* for chorus and orchestra dates from 1790; *Les Mais*, a comic ariette, from 1791; and a symphony entitled *Ça ira ça ira*, from 1792.

His creative output included a vast amount of music: concertos, chamber music, organ and harpsichord pieces, Masses, motets, cantatas, vaudevilles, and theater works (ballets, pantomimes, and comic scenes). And in addition to the music, Corrette produced a number and range of method books that will doubtless remain unmatched: for flute (1735), organ (1737), violin (1738), cello (1741 and 1766), viol (1748), harpsichord (1749), accompaniment (1753 and 1754), voice (1758 and 1768), guitar (1762 and 1763), mandolin (1772), string bass (1773), harp (1774), oboe and bassoon (1776), viola (1781), vielle (1783), and recorder (1784). These methods were extremely successful: the flute method went into four editions, the violin method into three, and several others into two; the vielle method was re-edited in 1825.

It is impossible to understand the career or the music of Michel Corrette without grasping the nature of the musical spheres in which he worked. This is not easy to do, however, for he worked within systems unique to Paris and without parallel elsewhere. There was of course the royal court, with a nucleus of musicians which was augmented for special occasions. The court of Corrette's youth was that of Louis XV, who, unlike his predecessor, was no supporter of the arts. Born only a year after Corrette, the King came to the throne as a boy of five. The Regency (1715–23) saw the development of competing mini-courts, of which the most dazzling was Sceaux, residence of the Duc du Maine, the favorite son of Louis XIV (by his mistress Marie de Montespan). The Duchesse, Anne-Louise de Bourbon-Condé, maintained an extensive musical establishment that included the incomparable Jean-Joseph Mouret (1682–1738), the chief composer of the most famous musical productions of the Regency. These were staged cantatas, ballets, and other divertissements that were called "Les Grandes Nuits de Sceaux." From 1718 on, Mouret was also involved with the Comédie-Italienne and the Opéra-Comique, for which he did his most important work.

As the cultural leadership of the royal court waned, the satellite courts attained greater vitality, and musical excellence reached outward toward the people. Beyond the court and the Opéra were the theaters of the great fairs of Paris. It was in these theaters that Corrette made his start, and his success reached its peak at the Opéra-Comique.

Public fairs were as old as public markets. Early twentieth-century American carnivals and county fairs suggest something of the early entertainments given by troupes of acrobats, magicians, mimes, and other performers who roamed Europe, appearing wherever they might get paid, whether at castle or town. This tradition expanded in Paris, where two great annual fairs spanned the year: from February 3, the Foire Saint-Germain, and from August 9, the Foire Saint-Laurent. There a substantial, well-to-do middle class could emulate the satellite courts. They would become one of the most knowing and appreciative audiences that ever attended public performances.

Early offerings, advertised by posted announcements, tended to emphasize spectacle, chiefly ropedancers and magicians. One for the Great Scot was typical:

We offer you daily the same entertainments that have been presented to His Most Christian Majesty, to all the Court, and to all the Crowned Heads of Europe and Asia. The Great Scot will drink an incredible amount of water, then convert it into all sorts of wine, milk, beer, ink, and colognes of several scents.

He will also perform the following Marvels:

He will bring forth from his mouth a salad as fresh as those sold at La Halle, two platefuls of live fish; roses, carnations, tulips, and other flowers as lovely and fresh as those growing in springtime gardens; and also live birds, three or four hundred gold pieces, lace and embroidered ties and cuffs, ribbons, and a thousand other inexplicable curiosities that surpass the imagination.

You will also see a ropedancer you will admire for his surprising leaps and postures, in addition to which his Italian Troupe are preparing to give each day a new and most amusing FARCE . . .

[Performances] will begin promptly at four o'clock. They will be held in the rue Mazarin at the Tennis Court at the Royal Palace, at the moat of the Faubourg Saint-Germain.[2]

A later announcement describes a more solid offering:

### The Troupe of All Pleasures,

After several delays, is finally ready to present during the Fair at Saint-Germain LASNE DE LUCIEN, or the LUDICROUS TRAVELER, a new Comedy, with a number of scene changes and surprising machines; and, offering his latest attractions, M. Langvicher, exclusive ropedancer to the KINGS of France and England, promises to mix dangerous leaps and extraordinary postures in a jig deserving the admiration of all Paris.[3]

A theater had now been built—the Théâtre de la Foire Saint-Germain, which opened in 1715, when Corrette was six—and a regular musical establishment was necessary. In 1718, however, the theater was suppressed except for rope-dancers and puppets in one skirmish in a long battle for control of public enter-tainments; but by 1721 it had reopened, "protected by persons of distinction."[4] The producers of plays with music now called their company the Opéra-Co-mique. They had been granted a license to present at the fairs "theatrical pro-ductions including song, dance, and orchestral music under the name *opéras-comiques*."[5] The connection between the fairs and the company remained strong: "Opéra-comique," wrote Voltaire, is "nothing but the kind of produc-tion, glorified, that you would see at the fair."[6]

Here was Corrette's milieu, here his public, to whom he directed his creative efforts—music and methods alike. He spoke to the amateurs who attended the Théâtre de la Foire and the Opéra-Comique. These were unique concepts and unique audiences. An understanding of this uniqueness is essential to under-standing the work of Michel Corrette.

Although the Opéra-Comique did occasionally present an opéra bouffe that we might call "comedy" in the modern sense ("farce" is probably a better term), the term "comedy" must be construed, as it was then, to designate a theater piece in vernacular prose with interspersed lyrics, dealing with everyday per-sons in everyday situations, with solo song and the expectation of a happy ending. The form was opposed not only to tragedy but to grand opera, which shared with tragedy the vital elements of a theater piece in formal, poetic dic-tion (in elegant Italian, to be precise), dealing with gods and exalted personages in heroic, highly dramatic stories, and which in addition featured choral as well as solo song, and the expectation of a tragic ending.

These distinctions unfolded during the eighteenth century. They were al-ready developing by the time Corrette began to compose skits and short scenes (both called *vaudevilles*) and concertos for the fairs and the Opéra-Comique. Concertos were performed between acts at the Opéra-Comique, and those of Corrette, the most successful of such works, were published as *concertos co-miques*. The title had nothing to do with their musical content, but only with their place of performance.

It is probable that Corrette's audiences were more discriminating than those of the court. In early eighteenth-century Paris, with a population of 800,000, more books on music were published than in mid-twentieth-century New York, with a population of 8,000,000. These books went into many editions. Accounts of the performing and composing of sonatas by amateurs indicate that they were music lovers of the best kind—literate, involved in the making of music themselves, and eager to assess new works.

It was for these knowledgeable and willing citizens that most of Corrette's method books were written. The harpsichord method bears the title:

*Les amusements du Parnasse* [which can be translated as "Heavenly Recreations" as well as "The Amusements of Parnassus"]: a short and easy method for learning to play the harpsichord, with beautiful and stylish airs in which fingerings are given for beginners together with the principles of music.

Such a title is clearly directed to the amateur who is interested in a good but easily undertaken study and, of course, in the latest stylish airs. Corrette issued eight volumes in this series between 1749 and 1772. His flute and violin methods (1735[7] and 1738) have similar titles and aims.

The methods testify to Corrette's lively mind, and have proved useful to scholars because they contain an abundance of historical and interpretative detail. It is from the harpsichord method on accompaniment, for example, that we learn how Louis XIV, asking to hear the sonatas of Corelli, had them sung to him by court singers because no French violinist could negotiate their difficulties.[8] Corrette's music similarly attests to a lively mind and also to a respect for his audiences, who he assumed had wide-ranging interests and knowledgeable taste in music.

Not all Corrette's works were composed for Foire/Opéra-Comique productions. His considerable output included important contributions to the literature of organ music, the cantata, sacred choral music (a Te Deum in 1752; *Trois Leçons de Ténèbres* in 1784), chamber music, and music for the harpsichord. Many of these speak of Corrette's consciousness of the new in music and in the world: his *Six Symphonies en Quatuor contenant les plus beaux Noëls Français et Etrangers* of 1771 are modern not only in their four-voice texture but in the use of carols of countries other than France, including one designated "American."[9] He also composed one of the first of the "battle pieces," a form that would achieve great popularity in Franz Kotzwara's *Battle of Prague* (1788) and James Hewitt's *Battle of Trenton* (c. 1800). Corrette's work, published in 1779, was certainly up to date, being entitled *Divertissements for Harpsichord or Pianoforte, containing Echos of Boston and Victory in a Naval Battle*. And his *Pièces pour l'orgue dans un genre nouveau* date from 1787, his seventy-eighth year.

Corrette's vocal music was also well appreciated, though as he grew older he was less modern in vocal idiom—except in parodies. His work ran a gamut of accompanying instruments as well as vocal forms: songs, airs, and cantatas with basso continuo; songs with guitar (in tablature); cantatilles with "simphonie," ariettes with violin and harpsichord or harp; and some vaudevilles in five parts.

Today, however, Corrette is chiefly known for the *concertos comiques*. These too were modern. His opus 3—concertos for three violins, oboes, or flutes with basso continuo (1728)—is generally recognized as comprising the first French concertos in the new Italian style. In fact, Corrette's music was a blend of French, Italian, and (even more modern) German elements; the exercises of the violin method[1] are drawn in surprising number from German sources—surprising, considering the almost total association of the violin with Italy on the part of modern scholars. Yet it was in Germany, with such composers as Heinrich Biber, that scordatura reached its apogee. Corrette discussed this device in his method; he taught fourth position on all strings, and up to seventh position on the E string.

For the twentieth-century historian, Corrette is more interesting by virtue of his experiments in the coming classical style. The concerto was a major form in such experimentation. Not always a concerto grosso and never in the modern

4

sense orchestral, it was most often—in France, but frequently even with Vivaldi—a chamber work for any combination of instruments, probing their capacities separately and together. In Austria chamber concertos were called divertimenti until they settled into standard types such as the string quartet and piano trio late in the century.

Corrette was inventive in creating musical forms. Even when dealing with "folk" tunes, Corrette created viable musical forms, which were energized by the Italian musical heritage from his father and focused by the German consciousness of a need for stylistic synthesis (so powerfully stated by both Quantz and Telemann, whom Corrette admired) and by his appreciative Parisian public.

More recondite styles were also in the grasp of this master: the duets of 1739[11] display a polythematic structure that is in some ways already fully classical, combining and justifying disparate elements in a single movement with even some suggestion of development. These duets are amazing works, fully realized without the bass, ready for two skilled violinists or flautists to bring them to life again. These are no pretty pieces for amateurs, but meaty, demanding works that are still a challenge when played up to tempo (see note 14).

The same is true of the *Sonates pour le Clavecin avec un Accompagnement de Violon*, opus 25 (1742), sonatas for violin and harpsichord.[12] These are also difficult professional works, using the form begun by Dieupart and La Guerre and perfected in Mondonville's opus 3. Although the sonatas of Corrette's opus 25 are more thoroughly Italianate than those of Mondonville's opus 3, they are finely wrought, musically robust successors to it. Corrette's music may have influenced Mondonville's opus 5 (1748), which is also more Italianate, though Corrette's love of folk material led him to musettes and related $\frac{3}{8}$ slow *ariosi* (marked affettuoso) for middle movements—a French predilection.

Of the $\frac{2}{4}$ signature, which he used more than any other, Corrette wrote: " $\frac{2}{4}$ is the 2 time of the Italians. This signature is used often in Allegro and Presto [movements] of Sonatas and Concertos. One must play the eighths equal and dot the sixteenths—one must at times play these equal as well in Sonatas."[13]

The dotting refers to "notes inégales"—a jazzing of the rhythm in French music not clearly understood in modern times. Of the $\frac{6}{8}$ signature Corrette stipulated that in both French and Italian jigs "the eighths are to be played equally." He is silent concerning the sixteenths in the jig, but it seems clear that anyone playing "in jig time"—twelve sixteenths per second—is too busy to bother with dotting.[14]

Modern views of Michel Corrette are without exception fragmented; a thorough study of his work remains to be written. Such as they are, these modern views are of two basic types: those that judge his milieu and those that examine one facet of his production.

The first is perhaps triggered by the words "comique," "vaudeville," and "amusement," all of which, musicologically speaking, have fallen on hard days. This view simply notes Corrette's connection with the Opéra-Comique, his love of folk materials, and his tremendous public success—all suspect in hierarchical minds—and assigns him at once to a musical limbo, although (sometimes grudgingly) it acknowledges the tremendous value of the method books, which are clear and full of specific details not often found in such books. Further, this view's concentration on "theme"—always to be "improved" in performance[15]—

rather than on texture and motivation, leads to a skewed evaluation of a composer for whom texture and energy were primary.

The other view, held by those who have examined the music, is quite different. Dufourcq, in his preface to the first book of organ pieces, speaks of Corrette's double heritage of French and Italian sources (and his ten years of regular attendance at the Concert spirituel, a stronghold of the Italian concerto); points out that "the organ was declining"; and cites the courage of this young composer in trying "to bring new life to the organ and to get his numerous pupils and admirers interested in the esthetics of the organ." Dufourcq admits that Corrette leaped from one style to another with little restraint, joining new and old, but says that the music is "strong on life, drive, a certain sort of grandeur, some gaiety, an obvious fluency that shuns the fine precepts [of methodology] taught by the old masters." He finds this a work of youthful zest, of "an inquiring mind, one in search of a style which is not disregardful of contemporary discoveries," one hoping to shake up stodgy Church traditions a bit.[16]

Roger Cotte, who conducted a performance of Corrette's concerto for hurdy-gurdy, speaks of the virtuosity of Corrette, a virtuosity wedded to the idiom of the instruments he wrote for. The hurdy-gurdy concerto Corrette typically consigned to his best students in performance; Cotte cites the variety that the composer could achieve in this sometimes limited instrument.[17]

French musicologist Guy Lambert sums up such responses to Corrette's music in his notes for concertos for bassoons and flutes. After acknowledging the breadth of style and type in Corrette's music, he applauds the honors given this composer by his grateful countrymen who in 1734 made him a Grand Maitre des Chevaliers du Pivois, and in 1750 a Chevalier de l'Ordre de Christ. Corrette's concertos, says Lambert,

Alternate soloists and tutti with dazzling verve and a sort of inherent ferocity....

Let us add Corrette's high moral standards as another admirable trait in his character—generous and helpful, one of his main tasks in life was to help young artists (Campra, for example), and both by his example and his writings he stood for all that was good in the artistic life of the French people.[18]

## NOTES

[1]The following legal reference is the only one recorded for either of the Correttes in Paris: "Corrette, Michel, master of music, living in the rue St-Honoré. 1733, 8 January: age about 26. Son of Gaspard C., the late organist, and Marie Jourdain. Married to Marie Catherine Morize, age 22, [at the church of] Saint-Germain l'Auxerrois," quoted from *Musiciens de Paris, 1535–1792. Actes d'état civil d'après le fichier Laborde de la Bibliothèque Nationale*, ed., Yolande de Brossard, La Vie musicale sous les rois bourbons, no. 11 (Paris: Picard, 1965).

[2]Several notices are given, without dates, by Jules Bonnaissies in his *Spectacles forains et la Comédie-Française* (Paris, 1875), pp. 6, 7, 25, 26, and 27. These demonstrate the use of streets, courtyards, and theaters by the entrepreneurs, as well as the latter's international character, as for instance the Grand foreign troupe of Ropedancers and Tumblers, fresh from a performance for His Electoral Highness of Bavaria. The announcement quoted here is from p. 6.

[3]Bonnaissies, p. 7.

[4]Bonnaissies, p. 42.

[5]The quote, from the patent, is given by René Dumesnil in his article, "Opéra-comique," in the *Larousse de la Musique*, ed. Norbert Dufourcq (Paris: Larousse, 1957). The form is currently defined as "a play combining spoken passages with episodes that are sung."

[6]Dumesnil.

[7]David Fuller in *The New Grove Dictionary of Music and Musicians* gives 1742, but the *privilège* at the end of the work says 1735.

[8]Several quotes from this and the vocal text (including a facsimile of the very useful chart of vocal and instrumental ranges opposite p. 177) appear in David Tunley, *The Eighteenth Century French Cantata* (London: Dobson, 1974). The complete quotation is on p. 14.

[9]This volume.

[10]*L'Art de se perfectionner dans le Violon*, 1782.

[11]This volume.

[12]This volume.

[13]In the *Méthode pour apprendre aisément à jouer de la Flûte Traversière*, 1735; pp. 4–6 discuss meter signatures.

[14]For tempos Corrette sent his students to "Notes on the Chronometers of M. Loulié and M. Saveur." The tables of Michel d'Affilard, based on those of Saveur and published in 1705, give the gigue the tempo of ♩. =120 and the signature C as ♩ =72, which might suggest the same for $\frac{2}{4}$, in view of Corrette's associating $\frac{2}{4}$ with the French 2; if $\frac{2}{4}$ is the same beat as ¢, it is ♩ =120. These tables, along with comparisons with later tables, are given on pp. 347–49 of Wilfrid Mellers, *François Couperin and the French Classical Tradition* (London: Dobson, 1950).

[15]In *Le Parfait Maître à Chanter* of 1747 (p. 47), Corrette stated that "song without ornament renders the voice like an unpolished diamond." Translation by David Tunley, p. 38.

[16]*Premier Livre d'orgue de Michel Corrette, 1737, restitué par Norbert Dufourcq* (Paris: Bornemann, 1980).

[17]Cotte's comments are from the notes on the recording (Musical Heritage/ Arion MHS-4175). "Spectacular" virtuosity is also cited by Jean-François Paillard in his notes for Corrette's Divertissement, opus 7, played by two trumpets on Sine Qua Non/Erato SNQ-7776. A concerto in C major, *La choisy*, for French horn, was recorded in 1974 by the Société Française du Son; Edmond Leloir says that this "is considered to be the first French Concerto written for the horn," but he gives neither date nor opus number (PLE-009).

[18]Concertos for Woodwinds (Westminster, XWN-18694).

# CORRETTE ON THE VIOLIN
## *Gabriel Banat*

In an age devoted to specialization such as ours, a personality like Michel Corrette can be difficult to understand, let alone explain. The variety of instrumental and vocal fields in which he practiced and taught is staggering, even taking into account his long career, which spanned practically the entire eighteenth century. It is therefore remarkable that, in spite of this wide range of activities, Corrette's involvement with the violin was quite significant.

The period from 1738, when *L'Ecole d'Orphée*, his first violin method, was published, to 1782, when *L'Art de se perfectionner dans le Violon* appeared, was a time when the violin flourished and enjoyed immense popularity in France. From the low estate of an instrument considered vulgar, fit only for the dance band, it rose to become the darling of the highly civilized patrons of court and bourgeoisie. According to the records in the French National Archives for the year 1738, the violinists Guignon and Guillemain played ninety-six concerts at court, earning 576 livres, that is, 6 livres per concert. These two stars were representative of the Italian school of virtuosity recently introduced in France. The repertoire of this circle of violinist—composers simply bristled with inventions for the bow, in addition to the demands made on the agility of the left hand.

A glance through Corrette's violin methods is sufficient to convince us that the author had a comprehensive knowledge of these latest advances in violin technique. In *L'Ecole d'Orphée* Corrette bridged the gap between the style of the French dance players and the higher level of the *sonatistes* influenced by the Italian school. The former still used the French grip, with the thumb on the bow hair, and read their music with the G clef on the first staff (the soprano clef):

(*L'Ecole d'Orphée*,[1] page 7); and:

### Leçons
#### Pour apprendre a joüer du Violon
#### dans le goût François.

*Prélude.*

(*L'Ecole*, page 13; where P=*poussé*, T=*tiré*, up and down bows, respectively; A=open string)

But in the same volume Corrette also recommended holding the violin with the chin, in order to free the hand for shifting. This anticipated the technical demands in the collection of works by Italian and German virtuosos that Corrette assembled in his 1782 anthology, *L'Art de se perfectionner dans le Violon.* There, in the Preface, he says:

I have prepared little preludes in all the major and minor keys; after that I offer lessons, selected mostly from the best Italian authors, where I have used only those parts that seemed to me most suitable for study, and that can serve as general examples for the performance of all music, past and present.[2]

Later in the same Preface he admonishes: "I think it unnecessary to mention that one must not abandon a difficult passage before it is well known: that is the real manner of becoming a virtuoso as shown by the Locatellis, Tartinis, 'le grand Claire [Leclair].' etc."[3] This, Corrette's second violin method, contains an important collection of excerpts from the repertoire of the period. Its demands include skills made possible by the evolution of the modern bow, which was an accomplished fact by the 1780s. Corrette's choices of technically challenging passages, mostly from the Italian school of virtuosos, with his own indications for fingerings meticulously worked out, prove not only that he was familiar with these achievements in violinistic skill, but also that he must have played and taught at that level himself. Even in his earlier violin method he teaches up to the seventh position:

### Exemple sur la Chanterelle.

*2ᵉ position.  3ᵉ position.  4ᵉ position.  5ᵉ position.  6ᵉ position.  7ᵉ position.*

*ainsi pour monter à l'ut dessous la Chanterelle il faut mettre le premier doigt sur le Sol et pour aller au Ré le premier doigt sur le La, La même observation pour les autres positions.*

(*L'Ecole*, page 37).

It is surprising, then, that Corrette's own musical compositions, at least those still available to us, are technically unpretentious. Actually, Corrette seems to take a slightly disdainful view of virtuosity, judging from a sentence in the Preface to *L'Art*: "I offer . . . the fingering most often used to climb to the top of the fingerboard in order to achieve tours de force: this is the name ordinarily given to that kind of feat by the amateurs."[4]

Another, more tangible reason for his restraint *vis-à-vis* technical virtuosity might be found in the pragmatic nature of his character. Witness the twenty teaching methods he wrote and his army of students, all of which aroused the open jealousy of his colleagues and even some of his friends.[5] The accessible nature of his compositions and his teaching methods for such a variety of instruments together suggest a dedicated, perhaps even compulsive proliferator of music. Whether his motivation was altruistic or materialistic, whether he was a missionary or a salesman of musicianship, is unimportant. Evidently it was more important to him that as many people as he could reach be able to play his music. It appears that competing with the virtuoso composers of the day—Guignon, Guillemain, and others—on their own turf, would have put his works beyond the reach of too many people.

Fortunately, his desire for acceptance by the public at large did not prevent Corrette from being receptive to new forms or ideas. He followed Mondonville very closely in writing *clavecin* sonatas with an independent obligato violin part: he wrote his *Sonates pour le Clavecin avec un Accompagnement de Violon*, opus 25, in 1742, soon after Mondonville had perfected this form, and introduced *cordes ravalées* (scordatura, or altered tuning) to the French school, which prompted Tremais, Lemaire, Guillemain, and other virtuosos to employ it in their works.

Contrasting with this kind of sophistication is Corrette's use of popular and folk tunes from Paris and the countryside in his twenty-five *concertos comiques*. These pieces, based on traditional folk materials, as well as on topical hit tunes of the day, offer their pleasures without demanding more skill than the average amateur or Sunday fiddler could muster. They were written for four- or five-part ensembles. Their titles indicate that they were meant to be played by an interchangeable array of instruments including flutes, oboes, trumpets, mandolins, musettes (or bagpipes), and of course strings. However, all eight of the concertos reproduced in this volume clearly indicate the violin as the first choice of instrument. Except in two concertos where the viola is added, the concertos are scored for three violins and a continuo. In the continuo, the bass part should be played on the cello.

Corrette sings the praises of the violoncello most eloquently in his 1741 method,[6] which he claims to be the first for that instrument. Writing about its advantages over the string bass or the viola da gamba, he says: "The harmonious tone of the violoncello being more audible than that of any other bass instrument, it must be the one holding the reins of the concerto, the treble instruments being more inclined toward rushing the time, in a piece."[7] Later in the same work, he mentions that, *"présentement à la musique de roi, à l'Opéra et dans les concerts, c'est le violoncelle qui joue la basse continue."*[8] His instruction calling for violoncello in the "Amoroso" of the *Marche du Huron* also confirms this. In all of these works the first violin part is generally soloistic, with assistance from the second violin, while the third is used as a "tutti" player.

Whether the word "comique" in the title refers to the use of these concertos as entr'actes of the Opéra-Comique, as some seem to think, or alludes to their amusing character, is an open question. The original lyrics of the songs quoted in the concertos may have referred to topical subjects with humorous connotations for the well-informed public of that day.[9] Another clue might be the legend on the title page of the first concerto, *Le Mirliton*, proclaiming it "a work good for melancholics."

The *Noëls*, although suitable for multiple players in each part, are perfect for a string quartet, a brand new idea in France at this time. While quite a bit more difficult than the *concertos comiques*, they present no real challenge to the skilled player. They are fashioned on a garland of French and foreign Christmas carols that should be a veritable gold mine for the thematic archivist or musical geographer.

The *VI Duetti à Due Violini*, opus 23, and the *Sonates pour le Clavecin avec un Accompagnement de Violon*, opus 25 (both in this volume), are representative of Corrette's conventional works. Unlike his other set of duos opus 2,[10] which was interchangeable for either flutes or violins, this set of duos is primarily written for violins. The two parts, equal and alternating in taking the lead, produce some of the most beguiling effects of musicianship and instrumental color, but are always fashioned with the simplest possible means at hand. Even the sonatas for the *clavecin*—though much more advanced technically than the preceding works, and with a violin part more active than Mondonville's opus 3[11]—avoid any tours de force. The first three can be played entirely in the first position, and while the keyboard part calls for trills, mordents, and turns, the violin part is satisfied with the simple trill (*t*). The presto of the fourth sonata goes up to the fourth position for only one bar. The fifth sonata, *Les Jeux Olympiques*, offers some arpeggios, as does the programmatic sixth sonata, *Les Voyages d'Ulysse*. Written as chords, they are of course to be arpeggiated:

(opus 25, page 33, line 1, bars 4–6). The passage describing Ulysses' swim to the isle of Calypso does contain some *pincé* (mordents), and the Giga *Le Départ d'Ulysse*, gets some healthy chords (non-arpeggiated):

(page 37, line 1, bars 9–10).

In all these works, both the "popular" and the "serious," Corrette achieves charming music without resorting to the arsenal of instrumental effects that were known and available to him. Some of these, all mentioned in his methods, are the use of arpeggio, vibrato, *batteries*, scordatura, staccato *lié*, scales in thirds, stretching to tenths, tours de force to tenth position, and so on. In the preface to *L'Art*, Corrette gives us an idea of the kind of player he had in mind for that volume: "I assume that one is capable of playing a part in a concerto, but one must not be satisfied with that. To achieve excellence on the violin, one must also be able to play solos such as sonatas, concertos, or *symphonies concertantes*, in which many composers excel at present."[12]

*L'Ecole d'Orphée*, the earlier work, was meant to teach a less advanced, no doubt larger group of fledgling violinists, the fashion of music having attracted droves of aspiring dilettantes from the titled nobility as well as the newly rich bourgeoisie. It is interesting that *L'Ecole* included music with the G clef on the first stave, in the "French style," a musical notation considered outdated after about 1715. It also contained several pieces by Corrette set in scordatura:

(*L'Ecole*, page 40, line 1; note that the D string is tuned down a minor third. Note further that unlike in *L'Art*, all the musical examples in this work are by Corrette himself.)

*L'Ecole d'Orphée* followed Pierre Dupont's method, *Principes de Violon* (1718), by twenty years. After that, Corrette's work stood alone until 1772 when the admirable *Principes du Violon* by Abbé le Fils appeared. The importance of Corrette's *L'Art de se perfectionner dans le Violon* was surpassed only by Jean Baptiste Cartier's collection *L'Art du Violon* of 1798. Corrette's *L'Art* contains a collection of concerto and sonata movements ranging from the still famous to some forgotten or lost works. Even familiar works by composers like Vivaldi or Locatelli are of interest here, thanks to comments and contemporary fingerings provided by Corrette. Of the vast number of works by lesser known composers in the anthology, only a handful have found their way into the repertoire at any given time. We would have no knowledge of much of this treasury but for Corrette's work.

Corrette's remarkable idea of fashioning concertos and quartets with folk or popular materials became his most fortuitous medium, anticipating a twentieth-century trend. It may be that he was attracted to this mode by a kind of patriotic reaction against the domination of the Paris scene by the Italianate virtuosos. While his admiration for them as a violinist and teacher remained undiminished, as a composer he turned to materials essentially French, or popular, as an antidote. In his conventional works, too, Corrette steered away from the virtuoso models. Instead, he seems to have been influenced by Handel or Telemann, whom we know he admired. While J.S.Bach, in his incomparable solo sonatas and partitas succeeded in marrying great music to the technical feats of the earlier German violinists (e.g., Biber and Walther), Handel and Telemann thought more in musical and less in instrumental terms than Bach. This allowed for interchangeability of instruments but precluded writing idiomatically for a particular instrument such as the violin. Corrette seems to have followed their example.

There is a curious dichotomy between Corrette the theorist and teacher of the violin, and Corrette the composer of music for the violin. As a teacher, Corrette published and taught up to the highest level of the considerable technical virtuosity of his era. But as a composer he eschewed all tours de force in both of his distinct styles—the popular or folk of the *Noëls* and *concertos comiques* on the one hand, and the conventional style of the sonatas on the other. It is not clear whether he was motivated in this by patriotism, a desire for wide popularity, admiration for the instrumental simplicity of his German models, or all of these. That and other questions will be answered only by a comprehensive study of the man, yet to come.

Corrette's importance as a pedagogue and a chronicler of the violin has been taken for granted. So was the judgment of one of his contemporaries who said that "Corrette's music died before him."[13] The present revival of his music in print and on recordings is a somewhat tardy but firm reprieve from that verdict. In the end, the simple charm of his music outlived the dazzling instrumental skill of so many of his contemporaries.

*J'exerce dans ma solitude,*  
*Différens traits de Concerto ;*  
*Qu'on est charmé de son étude,*  
*Quand le public nous dit Bravo.*

*Par une illusion nouvelle,*  
*Non, comme Icare audacieux,*  
*Sur la Brillante chanterelle,*  
*Je vole jusque dans les cieux.*

(*L'Art*, frontispiece). Or in free English translation:

> Practicing concerto parts
> Must be done in solitude
> How charming then it is to hear
> Bravos from the multitude.
>
> Icarus in his bold attempt
> Failed to reach the sky.
> I can enter Paradise
> On my E-string high.[14]

*Bon voyage, Maître!*

*Excerpts from*

## L'ART DE SE PERFECTIONNER DANS LE VIOLON[15]

The following examples were selected by the editor to illustrate Corrette's approach to performance, with emphasis on the authentic fingerings of the period. D indicates shifting up, G indicates shifting down, and A indicates open string. Strings are indicated by the number of dots: E string, one dot; A string, two dots; and so on.

(*L'Art*, page 53, lines 1 and 2). Note the repeated downshifting on the beat with the fourth finger:

(*L'Art*, page 54, line 9, bars 1-5). First finger is used for shifting up. Observe also in *La Cetra*:

(*L'Art*, page 55, lines 1–3). Note the manner of descent from the high position—crossing strings rather than stretching down—in line 3 of this example.

Corrette explains the *batterie* from Vivaldi's opus 7—

(*L'Art*, page 49, line 2, bars 1–2)—in the following fashion:

(*L'Art*, page 49, line 10, bar 6).

His respect for Locatelli's ability to stretch the fourth finger is illustrated in a caprice from opus 10 of that master:

(*L'Art*, page 69, line 4). Note the use of the third and fourth fingers on the first double stop. The whole section is to be played in the first position, with the fourth-finger stretch that Corrette considered typical of Locatelli's technique.

An example from Saccia, opus 1,

(*L'Art*, page 39, line 10) reiterates a preference for downshifting with the whole hand, leading with the fourth finger, a practice known to modern students from Gaviniès' *Matinales*. This is also true in the following lines by the renowned Somis, teacher of Leclair:

(*L'Art*, page 41, lines 7–8). Note the use of the open E string for downshifting. This is also demonstrated in a brilliant passage, mostly in the sixth position with stretches for the fourth finger, from Maurini, opus 1:

(*L'Art*, page 29, lines 1–5). Note that the second finger in line 3, bar 2, is a misprint; the third finger should be indicated.

The use of fifths played with the fourth finger—not the most comfortable way to do it—might have been less taxing on the eighteenth-century instrument with its lower bridge and all gut strings. Note the example by Facco, opus 1:

(*L'Art*, page 24, lines 1–3).

Two places in the *Point d'Orgue*, or cadenzas, by Castrucci, call for the full shift from fourth to first finger generally considered "modern":

(*L'Art*, page 16, line 3, bar 3, to the end of line 4).

The Preface to *L'Art* contains some performance notes by Corrette:

*Sur des notes longues il faut faire des pincés, même sur des Simples noirs, c'est ce qui rend le jeu brillant :*

(*L'Art*, page 4). "We must play mordents on the long notes, even on the quarter notes; that makes the performance brilliant." Further we read:

*Ce port de voix se fait quelquefois dans les adagio plus long que la note même qui le suit au reste l'usage et le bon goût doivent déterminer .*

*Pour enfler le Son sur une note longue, il faut commencer par conduire avec douceur l'archet sur la corde, ensuite le fortifier au milieu selon la valeur de la note et finir comme on a commencé en balançant un peu le doigt sur la corde*

(*L'Art*, pages 4–5). "Sometimes in adagios the grace note [ascending] is to be played longer than the main note: for the rest, custom and good taste must be your guide. To swell the sound on a long note, the bow must start softly, strengthen in the middle according to the value of the note and finish as it started, balancing the finger a little on the string [vibrato]."

There is a reference to Locatelli's *Caprices* in connection with stretching in intervals of tenths:

17

*Ceux qui ont le petit doigt cour ne peuvent guerres faire l'intervalle de dixiéme comme le Si sur la deuxieme corde et Ré sur la Chanterelle.*

*(Voyes le menuet de Zarth page 56)*

*Dans les caprices de Locatelli il y a souvent de ces sortes de passages, attendu que cet auteur alloit en Ré sur la Chanterelle sans demancher ce que tous les Violons ne peuvent pas faire quoique très habile d'ailleurs*

(*L'Art*, page 5). "Those [players] with short little fingers cannot reach a tenth like B on the second string and D on the E. . . . In Locatelli's *Caprices* such passages often occur, since this composer could reach the D on the E string without shifting, a [feat] that not all Violins [violinists] are capable of, although otherwise quite able."

## NOTES ON CORRETTE'S PERFORMANCE

On page 7 of *L'Art* Corrette calls for *notes égales*:

(line 8, bar 1). This is a reference to the "rule of the unequal notes," a much debated issue. Corrette characterizes this technique in a somewhat oversimplified instruction for *contredances angloises* published in 1740 as "dotting the quavers two by two."[16] In Chapter IV of *L'Ecole* he devotes several pages to this matter (see *L'Ecole*, pages 3–5).

Boyden summarizes Corrette's rules on this subject in the following table:

| Signature: | |
|---|---|
| 2 (as in *rigaudons, branles, gavottes, bourrées*, etc.) ₵, 6/4 3 (as in *menuets, sarabandes, courantes*, etc.) | The second of two eighths is played shorter (i.e. long-short inequality). |
| C (often in church music and Italian music) 2/4 (common in Italian music, in *vivace, presto*, and in *ariettes*) | Eighths played equally; the second of two sixteenths shorter. |
| 3/4, 3/8 3/2 | The second of two quarters is played shorter. |

(Boyden, *The History of Violin Playing*, page 473).[17]

On the trill, Corrette says:

18

## Des Cadences.

La Cadence se prepare toujours par la notte Superieure et se marque par un t. ou +

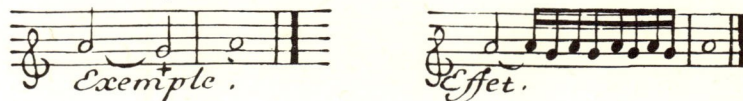

Exemple.     Effet.

(*L'Ecole*, page 11).

Note that in the concertos the placement of dynamic marks sometimes differs from part to part. Note that + and *t* are both used to indicate "cadence" (trill); ♭ or ♯ is sometimes used to indicate ♮ according to the archaic custom. ⌒⌒ is used for first and second endings, in other cases both versions appear in the measure without any explanation. Passages in the *concertos comiques* appearing as octaves indicate that should a flute be substituted for the violin, the higher register is to be played.

On swelling the sound with the bow, Corrette observes:

Dans les sarabandes, Adagio, Largo ; et autres Pieces de goût. il faut faire les Rondes, Blanches, et Noires avec de grands Coups d'Archet et enfler les sons sur la fin. A.B. mais pour les finalles et terminaisons de chants, il faut Commencer le coup d'Archet avec douceur le fortifier au milieu et le finir en mourant C.D.E. ce coup d'Archet fait un tres bel effet.

Sarabande

(*L'Ecole*, page 34). "Whole notes, half notes and quarter notes must be played with large strokes of the bow, swelling the sound toward the end. But for endings, they must swell in the middle, dying away at the end as marked by C, D, and E. This makes a very nice effect."

Regarding dynamics, Corrette cautions:

Il faut que le Violon joue a demi jeu.
Violino.

SONATA I.

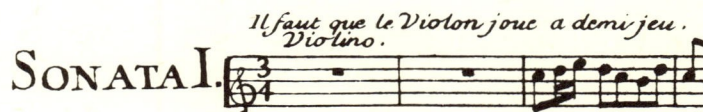

(*Sonates pour le Clavecin avec un Accompagnement de Violon*, opus 25, page 2, line 1). This instruction asking for the violin to play mezza voce is a clear indication that covering the harpsichord is not a problem of recent origin. There is ample

19

evidence that the violin had to deal with this long before its transformation in the nineteenth century.

Finally, he offers models for arpeggios, *pincé* (or mordents), and *port de voix* (or grace notes):

(*L'Ecole*, page 35, lines 6–9).

(*L'Ecole*, page 35, line 10).

## ERRATA

### *Violino Primo*

Six Symphonies en Quatuor

Page 1, line 1, bar 2: Final three sixteenths should possibly be in unison with the other parts as .

Page 1, line 4, bar 6: Last note is probably B♭, not A.

Page 2, line 11, last bar: "Piano" and "crescendo" are missing.

Page 3: Dynamics in this part are missing from alto and organo parts.

Page 3, line 7, bars 4 and 5: Slur as in violino secondo.

Page 3, line 11, bar 8: "Forte" is probably missing here.

Page 3, line 12: Note "Andante" in other parts.

Page 4, line 11, last bar: The "da capo" and fermata are missing.

Page 5, line 4, bar 4: "Allegro" is missing.

Page 5, line 5, bar 3: Read either A or F♯ for the second note to agree with the bass.

Page 5, line 10, bars 2 and 6: Read F♯ throughout.

Page 5, line 11, last bar; line 12, bar 8: Read F♮.

Page 5, line 12, bar 12, beat 1: Read G, B, C.

Page 5, line 14, bar 1: For second note read A as in bar 9.

Page 5, line 14, last bar: Second note of the triplet is missing; possibly G.
Page 6, lines 6–8: Violino secondo has slurs throughout.
Page 7, line 1, last bar: Read B♮.
Page 7, line 8, bar 14: Only this part has a repeat.
Page 8, line 10, bar 11: First note is probably E or A.
Page 9, line 6, bar 8: The fermata is missing.
Page 9, line 8, last bar: The "da capo" belongs one line higher.
Page 11, line 6, bar 3: Probably four D's rather than the final E, to be in unison with the violino secondo.

Le Mirliton
Page 3, line 5, bars 5 and 6: Probably dotted as before.
Page 3, line 7, bar 2: Read C♮ in the fourth beat.

Les Pantins
Page 2, line 1: "Allegro" is missing.
Page 2, line 5, bar 4: Read F♯.
Page 3, line 1: Note "Adagio" in other parts.

La Touriere
Page 3, line 6, bar 6: Grace note is B, not C.

XIX Concerto Comique
Page 2, line 4, bars 1 and 5: *t* on C♯.
Page 2, line 4, bar 3: *t* on B.

La Marche du Huron
Page 2, line 8, bar 6: Sixteenth rest belongs on left side of repeat.

Les Sauvages
Page 2, last line, last bar: "Da capo" is missing.
Page 3, line 11, bar 3: Read B♮.

*Violino Secondo*

Six Symphonies en Quatuor
Page 4, line 8: Note a discrepancy in dynamics.
Page 6, line 2, bar 11: "Allegro" is missing.
Page 6, lines 6 and 8: The "da capo" and "fine" are missing as in violino primo.
Page 6, line 8, bars 10 and 18: Read F♮.
Page 6, line 11: "Allegro" is missing.
Page 7, line 5, bar 5: Should be dotted half note.
Page 7, line 10, bar 3: Read C♯, E, D, C♯ for second half.
Page 7, line 12, bar 5: Fermatas are missing in other parts.
Page 8, line 8, bar 13: "Allegro" is missing.
Page 8, last line, bar 5: Naturals are missing to cancel A major signature.
Page 9, line 8, bar 3: The fermata is missing.

Page 9, line 13, bar 9: First note is probably D.
Page 9, last line, bar 6: Read C♯.

Le Mirliton.
Page 2, line 1, bar 2: For the fourth beat, read C♮.

La Touriere
Page 1, line 3, bar 2: Read F♯.
Page 1, line 3, bar 9: Second note is probably A.
Page 1, last line, bar 10: Read F♯.

La Marche du Huron
Page 1: "Allegro" is missing.

Les Sauvages
Page 1, line 5, bar 1: Read E♮.
Page 1, line 7, end: The "da capo" is missing.

## Violino Terzo

Le Mirliton
Page 1, line 5, bar 10: Probably B♭, E♭, G.
Page 2, line 1, bar 2: Fourth beat is C♮.
Page 2, line 1, bar 4: Second beat is a quarter rest.
Page 2, line 7, bar 11: "Tutti" is missing.
Page 2, line 9, bar 8: Read E♮.

La Marche du Huron
Page 1: "Allegro" is missing.
Page 1, line 10, bar 15: Second note is E.

Les Sauvages
Page 1, line 4, last bar: Read E♮.
Page 1, line 8, bar 4: The "da capo" is missing.

## Alto

Six Symphonies en Quatuor
Page 2, line 2, bar 7: One measure rest follows this bar.
Page 2, line 5, bar 11: Read C, not D.
Page 2, line 11, bar 1: Last note is G, not F.
Page 2, last line, bar 6: "Allegro" is missing.
Page 3, line 6, bar 5: Second note is A, not B.
Page 4, line 1: Dynamics found on other parts are missing here.
Page 4, line 2, bar 9: A is incorrect; a possible reading is B.
Page 4, line 13, bar 11: "Largo" is missing.
Page 5, line 1, last bar: Repeat sign is missing.
Page 5, lines 4–7: The "da capo" and "fine" are missing.
Page 5, line 9, bar 7: "Allegro" is missing.

Page 5, line 12, last bar: Probable reading is G, not A.
Page 6, line 2, bar 10: Last note is probably G, not F.
Page 6, line 3, bars 2 and 10: Probable reading is F♮.
Page 6, line 8, bar 2: Probable reading is A.
Page 6, line 9, bar 4: First note is probably A.
Page 6, lines 9 and 10: The fermatas are missing.
Page 6, line 11, bar 7; line 12, bar 5: Both measures should probably read A, B♭, A, A.
Page 7, line 8, bar 1: Second beat should probably be read as E, E.
Page 7, line 10: Read "Adagio," not "Allegro."

La Marche du Huron
Page 1: "Allegro" is missing.

Les Sauvages
Page 1, line 1: Second flat in key signature is missing in first and third movements.
Page 1, line 8: The "da capo" is missing; no repeat.

*Basso*

Le Mirliton
Page 2, line 1, bar 2: Read C♮ in the fourth beat.

Le Quadrille
Page 2, last line, bar 4: A possible reading for the middle note is G♯.
Page 2, last line, bar 10: Repeat sign is missing.

La Servante au Bon Tabac
Page 1, line 6, bar 5: Last note is B♭, not C.

XIX Concerto Comique
Page 2, line 6, bar 1: The fermata in the basso is valid for all parts.

*Organo*

Six Symphonies en Quatuor
Page 2, line 6, bar 6, Read B♮.
Page 2, line 9: "Piano" is missing.
Page 5, line 5: "Piano" is missing.
Page 5, last line, bar 4: Repeat sign is missing.
Page 7, line 1, bar 1: Last note is probably G.
Page 7, line 13, bar 12: Eighth rest is missing after repeat.
Page 8, line 9: "Allegro" is missing.
Page 9, line 8: The upbeat to bar 2 is probably E.
Page 9, line 8, bar 11: The fermata is missing.
Page 9, line 9: "Allegro" is missing.
Page 10, line 3, bar 3: Second note should be A.
Page 11, line 6, bar 4: Second note is probably B.

Le Mirliton
   Page 2, line 1, bar 2: read C♮ in the fourth beat.

Le Quadrille
   Page 2, line 11, bar 5: Middle note could possibly be G♯.

La Servante au Bon Tabac
   Dynamics are missing in basso and organo parts.
   Page 1, line 3, bar 5: Flat under the staff belongs with figures above.

XIX Concerto Comique
   Page 2, line 4, bar 8: *P* should be on bar 9 (not 8) in organo and basso.

Les Sauvages
   Page 1, line 9: "Andante" is missing.
   Page 2, line 1: "Allegro" is missing.
   Page 2, line 9, last bar; line 10, bar 4: Read F♮ in second half.

## VI Duetti

Page 6, beginning: Read either $\frac{2}{4}$ or $\frac{4}{8}$, not $\frac{2}{8}$.
Page 8, beginning: Read $\frac{6}{8}$, not $\frac{3}{8}$.
Page 17, system 5, line 2, bar 2: The first sixteenth of the fourth beat should be read D♯.
Page 26, end: Repeat for the entire piece must be an error since the work is a set of variations on a theme.

## Sonates pour le Clavecin

Page 2, system 4, bar 5 (clavecin, right hand): Read F♯.
Page 7, system 3, bar 4 (violin): Read F♯.
Page 8, system 1: Read $\frac{2}{4}$, not $\frac{4}{2}$.
Page 14, system 5, bar 2 (clavecin, right hand): Grace note is A♯.
Page 15, system 1, bar 2 (violin): ♯ is on B.
Page 16, system 1 (clavecin): Alternate accompaniment for repeat is given here.
Page 18, system 4, last bar (clavecin, right hand): Read D♯ in first half of measure.
Page 20, system 1, bars 7 and 8 (clavecin, right hand): Dot the third beats.
Page 20, system 2, last bar; system 3, bars 4 and 8 (clavecin, left hand): Too many rests.
Page 21, system 1, bar 4 (clavecin): Grace note is D♯.
Page 25, system 1, bar 10 (clavecin, right hand): Read C♯.
Page 26, system 3, bar 4 (clavecin, right hand): Read G♯ here.
Page 26, system 4, bar 2 (clavecin): Read G♯.
Page 27, system 3, bar 2 (clavecin, second beat; violin, third beat): Read G♮.
Page 32, system 3, bar 2 (clavecin, left hand): For the fourth beat, read F♯.
Page 34, system 3, bar 1 (clavecin, right hand): Reading is perhaps F♮.
Page 37, system 3, bar 4 (violin): Read G♯.

## NOTES

[1] *L'Ecole d'Orphée* (Paris, 1738), cited hereafter as *L'Ecole*. Reprinted by Minkoff Reprint, Geneva, 1973. All examples that appear in this volume from *L'Ecole* are reproduced by permission of Minkoff Reprint.

[2] *L'Art de se perfectionner dans le Violon* (Paris, 1782), p. 3; cited hereafter as *L'Art*. Reprinted by Minkoff Reprint, Geneva, 1973.

[3] Ibid., p.3.

[4] Ibid., p.1. "Amateur" is to be taken in the eighteenth-century sense of the word, not meaning "dilettante."

[5] Referring to his students, his friend Pierre Gaviniès coined the phrase *anachoretes (ânes à Corrette)*, a pun meaning "Corrette's donkeys [*Die Musik in Geschichte und Gegenwart*]." That Corrette had a sense of humor, too, is obvious from his fondness for little poems, or doggerels. One, at the end of *L'Art* (p. 91) suggests that those who find his lessons too difficult might play the number of a particular page on the Royal Lottery until either the page is mastered or the number wins a prize.

[6] *Méthode théorique et pratique pour apprendre en peu de tems le violoncelle dans sa perfection*, opus 24, 1741.

[7] Ibid., p. a.

[8] Ibid., p. 46.

[9] *Mirliton* (toy flute); *tourière* (lay sister charged with provisioning the convent); *pantins* (marionettes), and so on.

[10] *Sonates pour deux flûtes traversières sans Basse*, opus 2, 1727.

[11] *Pièces de Clavecin en Sonates avec accompagnement de Violon*, opus 3, 1734. Reprinted in Masters of the Violin, Vol. 5.

[12] *L'Art*, p. 1.

[13] Boisgelou, as cited by Eugène Borrel. See "Michel Corrette," *Die Musik in Geschichte und Gegenwart*. Kassel: Bärenreiter, 1955.

[14] Editor's translation.

[15] All examples that appear in this volume from *L'Art* are reproduced by permission of the Music Division, the Library of Congress. A list of composers cited in *L'Art* follows for reference purposes.

[16] "Michel Corrette," *The New Grove Dictionary of Music and Musicians*.

[17] Reproduced by permission of Oxford University Press.

## Composers Cited in Corrette's
## L'ART DE SE PERFECTIONNER DANS LE VIOLON

| | | |
|---|---|---|
| Abaco | Fesch | Ottoni |
| Alberti | Ferrari | Rasetti |
| Albinoni | Geminiani | Saccia |
| Birckenstok | Handel | Somis |
| Baustetter | Kenis | Tartini |
| Castrucc | Laurenti | Tessarini |
| Chinzer | Locatelli | Valentini |
| Conti | Maurini | Veracini |
| Corelli | Meck | Vivaldi |
| Degiardino | Moissi | Zarth |
| Facco | Nozeman | Zuccari |

## BIBLIOGRAPHY

L'Abbé le Fils. *Principes du violon*. Reprint of the 1772 edition. Geneva: Minkoff Reprint, 1976.

Baillot, Pierre. *L'Art du violon: Nouvelle méthode*. Paris: Heugel, 1834.

Bornet l'Aîné. *Nouvelle méthode de violon et de musique*. Paris: Chez l'Auteur, 1786.

Boyden, David D. *The History of Violin Playing from Its Origins to 1761 and Its Relationship to the Violin and Violin Music*. London: Oxford University Press, 1965.

Boyden, David D. ' The Violin and Its Technique in the 18th Century," *The Musical Quarterly*, XXXVI/1 (Jan. 1950), pp. 9–38.

*The British Union Catalogue of Early Music Printed before the Year 1801*. 2 vols., ed. Edith B. Schnapper. London: Butterworth's Scientific Publications, 1957.

Brook, Barry S. *La Symphonie française dans la seconde moitié du XVIIIᵉ siècle*. Université de Paris, Institut de Musicologie, no. 3. Paris, 1962.

Cartier, J. B. *L'Art du violon*. Facsimile of the 1803(?) edition. New York: Broude Brothers Limited, 1973.

Corrette, Michel. *L'Art de se perfectionner dans le violon*. Reprint of the 1782 edition. Geneva: Minkoff Reprint, 1973.

Corrette, Michel. *L'Ecole d'Orphée*. Reprint of the 1738 edition. Geneva: Minkoff Reprint, 1973.

Donington, Robert "A Problem of Inequality," *Musical Quarterly*, liii (1967), pp. 503–17.

Dorian, Frederick. *The History of Music in Performance: The Art of Musical Interpretation from the Renaissance to Our Day*. New York: W. W. Norton & Co., Inc., 1966.

Dupont, Pierre. *Principes de musique par demandes et par réponce*. Paris: Chez l'Auteur, 1718.

Fétis, François-Joseph. "Bailleux, Antoine," Vol. 1, p. 218; "Le Blanc, Hubert," Vol. 5, p. 238. *Biographie universelle des musiciens et bibliographie générale de la musique*. 2nd ed. 8 vols. Paris: Firmin Didot, 1867–70.

Gerber, Ernst. *Neues Historisch-biographisches Lexicon der Tonkünstler*. Leipzig: Künhel, 1812–14.

La Laurencie, Lionel de. *L'Ecole française de violon de Lully à Viotti*. 3 vols. Paris: Delagrave, 1922–24.

*Die Musik in Geschichte und Gegenwart*. Kassel: Bärenreiter, 1955.

Neumann, Frederick. *Baroque and Post-Baroque Ornamentation*. Princeton: Princeton University Press, 1978.

Neumann, Frederick. "The French Inégales, Quantz and Bach," *American Musicological Society Journal*, xviii (1965), pp. 313–56.

Newman, William S. *The Sonata in the Baroque Era*. New York: W. W. Norton & Co., Inc., 1972.

Pincherle, Marc. *Les Violonistes, compositeurs et virtuoses*. Paris: 1922.

Pougin, Arthur. *Le Violon, les violonistes et la musique de violon du XVI au XVIII siècle*. Paris: Fischbacher, 1924.

Quantz, Johann H. Joachim. *Versuch einer Anweisung die Flöte traversiere zu spielen* (1752). 2 vols. Trans. and with commentary by Edward Randolph Reilly, Ph. D. dissertation, University of Michigan, 1958.

Riemann, Hugo. "Etude," *Musik-Lexikon*. 11th ed. 2 vols., ed. Alfred Einstein. Berlin: Hesse, 1929.